PRAISE
# L OVE'S  G UEST

"Profound and simple . . . *In Love's Guest, Reflections of Inspiration and Wonder,* Marc Aronoff has uncovered a hidden spiritual gem, the meditations of St. Catherine of Genoa, a 15th Century lay Catholic mystic. Through his editorial art Marc has condensed St. Catherine's "Spiritual Dialogues" into a small mystical treasure accessible to all who wish to experience the soul piercing love of God."

**Deacon Jim McElroy, St. Mary, Mother of the Church Parish, Lee, MA**

"*Love's Guest* provides small but powerful phrases from the mystic Saint Catherine of Genoa who knew what it was to be possessed by love. Catherine's poetic insights will cause the reader to ponder the deepest form of love which comes from the ultimate Source of our being.  May these powerful words impact our world so in need of that love."

**Bishop John Stowe, OFM Conv., Bishop of Lexington**

"I knew nothing of St. Catherine of Genoa until I read Marc Aronoff's beautiful work *Love's Guest.*  This is not merely a hagiography or compilation of her inspired words, but also an insightful guide to prayer through and with this remarkable woman.  Regardless of your spirituality, Marc offers us a precious gift of experiencing and deepening God's love in our lives."

**Most Reverend Bishop William D. Byrne, Diocese of Springfield**

"Marc Aronoff lifts up St. Catherine of Genoa's *Spiritual Dialogues* in a modern English version. Enhanced by the artwork of Jan Richardson and his reflection guides, the book gracefully introduces the reader to this lesser known saint."

**Bonnie Thurston**

*"Love's Guest: Reflections of Inspiration and Wonder* offers insight into the awesome love that God has for each of us. Marc Aronoff introduces us to Saint Catherine of Genoa and her meditations. Our world is at a time of great unrest. This book is needed more now than ever as we read of God's Divine Love."

**Rev. Christopher J. Waitekus, Pastor, Saint Mary's Church Longmeadow, MA.**

"Down through the ages, human beings have waxed eloquently about the mystery we call 'love.' From St. Paul's beautiful reflection on the virtue of love in 1 Corinthians 13 to T. S. Eliot's 'The Love Song of J. Alfred Prufrock,' from St. John of the Cross's magnificent 'The Living Flame of Love,' to Shakespeare's *Romeo and Juliet*, there is no dearth of material on the 'greatest of the gifts.'

"With this in mind, we owe a debt of gratitude to Marc Aronoff, who has given us a remarkable glimpse into the writings of Saint Catherine of Genoa, a saint who rightfully takes her place in the pantheon of those who have deepened our understanding of love, with a focus on God's unfathomable love for us, his children. The pages of Mr. Aronoff's edited work come alive with St. Catherine's reflections, who clearly had the insight of a theologian and the heart of one possessed by God's love. Complemented by Jan Richardson's compelling artwork, this gem of a book is bound to capture your heart and enliven your spirit.

"St. John of the Cross famously said, 'In the evening of life, we will be judged on love alone.' No wonder Catherine of Genoa is a saint. And no wonder that Marc Aronoff has been inspired to make Catherine's spiritual journey accessible to the modern reader. St. Catherine wrote that 'A heart enamored of God … receives all that happens as from the hand of God, remaining in immovable peace.' May the peace of God abide in all who read and reflect on *Love's Guest.*"

**Most Reverend John C. Wester, Archbishop of Sante Fe, New Mexico**

"Inspirational, enlightening, wonderful."

**Fr. Brian McGrath S.T.L., Pastor of St. Mary's Parish, Lee MA**

# LOVE'S GUEST

## REFLECTIONS
### *of*
## INSPIRATION
### *&*
## WONDER

AN ANNOTATED SELECTION FROM
*The Spiritual Dialogues*
by
SAINT CATHERINE OF GENOA

UPDATED WITH MODERN ENGLISH AND A REFLECTION WORKBOOK

EDITED BY
MARC ARONOFF

ARTWORK BY
JAN RICHARDSON

Red Elixir
Rhinebeck, New York

Paperback ISBN 978-1-960090-26-3
eBook ISBN 978-1-960090-27-0
Audiobook ISBN 979-8-9878932-2-7

Library of Congress Control Number 2023913533

Book and cover design by Colin Rolfe

Red Elixir is an imprint of Monkfish Book Publishing Company

Red Elixir
22 East Market Street, Suite 304
Rhinebeck, New York 12572
(845) 876-4861
monkfishpublishing.com

*In memory of my mother, Joanne.*

# CONTENTS

# ARTWORK
## BY JAN RICHARDSON

**AUTHOR'S NOTE ON THE ARTWORK:**

I spent months searching for the correct illustrations to represent Saint Catherine of Genoa's prophetic words. When I saw the artwork of bestselling author and ordained minister Jan Richardson, I found what I was looking for—a unique clear voice through image, with an intangible clarity that also speaks of a journey through Love. I hope you may find the artwork equally meditative and inspiring.

# ACKNOWLEDGMENTS

This book is born on an inspiration to offer the words of Saint Catherine of Genoa to the general public. I would like to thank my spiritual community for the encouragement and feedback that has gone into creating this little book. In particular, I owe a debt of gratitude to Rev. Jennifer Kimball for her clarity, brevity, and support and to Martha Congdon, who suggested the title of the book from a passage I wrote in the Introduction. Special thanks to Rev. Bert Marshall for his feedback on my early drafts. I am deeply thankful for the articulate and soulful Leon Reyome, a member of Cathedral of the Divine, an outdoor church I frequent, (and the "wise man" I mention in the Introduction), for his depth of character and heart of truth in all our conversations. Thanks to Rose Scotch for reading the early drafts with a keen editorial eye. I offer thanks to Br. Paul at The Abbey at Gethsemane—our many conversations will be remembered for life. I am grateful for the gracious research support given by Bruce Gerstman. I would like to acknowledge the numerous spiritual teachers of mysticism and meditation, too many to mention, with whom I have met and studied over the years. Special thanks to my editor, Anne McGrath, at Red Elixir.

"If I could utter that Love of which my heart is full,
I think that every other heart would be inflamed,
however remote from Love it might be."

SAINT CATHERINE OF GENOA

# INTRODUCTION

Imagine Christianity in the 15th century: the political leaders of Christendom are at the height of corruption. Internal divisions are rife with intrigue as a dark hypocrisy transforms the Church with such ferocious force as to shake the foundation of all that is sacred. The crises of late medieval society and corruption of the clergy go hand in hand. Even so, among common folk and lay leaders alike, unpretentious Christians emerge who remain inspired and guided by the essence of Christ's teaching. It is notable that during this tumultuous time, Christianity gave birth to some of the century's greatest saints, whose lives exemplified powerful spiritual transformation, eventually touching the hearts of millions. We have Joan of Arc, Ignatius of Loyola, and many more. The mystic theologian Thomas Merton describes these saints as, "complete and simple signs of contradictions to worldliness and system, and convention, and prejudiced interest . . . In them you see clearly and movingly revealed what is not to be a mere rebel, but what is to be obedient to God as a sign of mercy, a revelation of truth and of power . . . meek and submissive instruments of God."[1] These were men and women devout in the light, love, and the Word of Christ. One such person, born 1447 into a distinguished God loving family in Genoa, Italy, was Caterina Fieschi Adorno.

A quiet, devout, exceedingly obedient girl, Caterina began her early years with a desire for prayer and steeped in a wonderful love of Christ's passion. At the age of 13 she attempted to enter a convent, but her young age precluded acceptance and she was turned away. She appeared to put the idea aside and enter a life of propriety, following her family's expectations.

At age 16 Catherine's parents arranged for her to marry a young Genoese nobleman who turned out to be a violent-tempered, faithless spendthrift. He left young Catherine a wife in deep misery and woe. Though praying often for change, Catherine spent the next ten years of her marriage in a submissive depression, with few glimpses of meaning or joy.

Twenty-six-year-old Catherine shared her sorrow with her sister, Limbania, a nun in the nearby convent of, Santa Maria delle Grazie. Her sister invited her to offer confession, which Catherine did, and after years of heartache, emotional harm, and exhaustion, a transformation occurred that changed not only her life, but the world around her.

At the moment of confession, Catherine was suddenly overwhelmed with the feeling that God was piercing her heart with such an intense love that she entered into a kind of Divine ecstasy, nearly passing out. At the same time, the priest who was receiving her confession was suddenly called away and upon his return he found Catherine crying. She was speechless and left the church abruptly. From that time forward, Catherine realized in the depth of her soul a love and calling that filled her with wonder and grace. This divine revelation, this feeling of Love, this passion for God, so transformed her that her husband was filled with profound humility and he, too, was inspired to change the course of his life toward God. History reveals both Catherine and her "born again" husband soon began ministering to the sick and poor during a time of plague, eventually ending their days living and working full-time at the Pammatone Hospital in Genoa. Catherine passed away on September 15th, 1510.

What allowed Catherine's "difficult" husband to change for the better? Why was he humbled to such a degree that he changed his manner and confessed his sins, including the fact that he had an illegitimate child? I imagine he experienced his wife's deepened love and conversion with awe, that he witnessed in her the expression of an ultimate power in this world—God manifest in the words and deeds of a human. Perhaps it was her tone or body language. A look in her eye. Her vulnerability. Her Words. Whatever it was, it caused him to change his manner of relating. This is the transformative power of mystical revelation; a compelling ability to enlighten the meanest, most ill-tempered, and deceitful of humans.

While certain people may come into our life offering clarity, inspiration, healing, and influence, I believe what happened to Catherine on that fateful day of her conversion is something that may happen to all of us. This *something* is rooted in our relationship with and potential for knowing *the mystical experience of God,* or as I sometimes relate, *the Divine,* in the fabric of life.

A relationship with God is nurtured through both a formal practice of meditation and prayer and our informal awareness and intention to allow for a mystical and ultimately spiritual union with God, moment-to-moment. Humans have an innate capacity to experience and awaken a transcendent experience of God. Our potential to experience the mystical reality of life speaks to the role of Divine Love in the world today: God's presence in our every breath, calling us to awaken, feel, and see with eyes of Christ. The French Jesuit Priest and writer Jean-Pierre de Caussade captures this feeling succinctly:

> Faith sees that Jesus Christ is present in everything and works through all history to the end of time; that every fraction of a second, every atom of matter contains a fragment of His hidden life and His secret activity.

In my work as a psychotherapist, I often ask new clients if they believe in a higher power or God. About 30 percent say yes, 30 percent say no, and 40 percent say, I don't know, maybe. Sometimes, I am told, "If I could only experience God, I would know . . ." I sometimes answer, "What if you could know—would you be interested in cultivating that experience?"

While the supernatural, mystical experience of God's Divine Love can happen at any moment for any reason, it is most often years in the making through the practice of deep prayer, meditation, trust, and surrender. Equally so, this revelation is not something we can chase, mimic, or *try too hard* to experience, "lest," as Catherine relates, "we should spoil it by making it our own." Rather, we are invited to trust, know, and believe we are being cared for and guided by God whether we "feel it" or not. Under the right conditions, with consistent faith, intuition, and creativity, our inborn seeds of spiritual consciousness may sprout.

I sometimes speak with clients about what I call "The God Chord" running through each of us—a chord of understanding beyond words, ever present and ever wise, connected to the divine. In a sense, all we have to do is remember and trust in this connection to cultivate the experience of God. This is no easy task. Much of modern life distracts us from our Divine nature. Human thought inevitably conditions and colors our reality based on our agendas—conscious or unconscious—experiences, traumas, family of origin, heart-breaks, betrayals, fears and any multitude of momentary or habitual quandaries of the temporal world. Yet, in the midst of human suffering and evolution, our God Chord, I believe, connects us to a sense of clarity and wisdom beyond all thought and circumstance, beyond words, beyond description, however challenging our life may be.

Consider this: at all times and all manner of human expression, our God Chord is with us day and night. Ever present. No Separation. It transcends time and space. No matter the outward circumstance. This is a certain faith and all we have to do is remember, as often as possible, this connection to the Divine. Whatever conditions influenced Catherine's husband to be vile also contained the seeds of his transformation toward faith and goodness.

Catherine's revelations may be described as a mystical experience of the Holy Spirit. While Catherine and her husband spent their remaining days helping the sick and infirm in Genoa, it must be noted, her life was not easy and her death, it is said, was prolonged and painful. Life following her conversion was no longer her own: being swept away by the Grace of God is not easy or comfortable. At times, Catherine felt the overwhelming intensity of her Union with God as a kind of "prison" of passion and visions. There were instances when she was so overwhelmed by Divine Ecstasy and Love that she was unable to speak or interact in "normal" ways. She would often fast for several weeks, particularly during Lent and Advent when she would take nothing but a small amount of water, vinegar, and ground salt. During the penitential weeks around Easter and Christmas, she sought to receive the eucharist— typically reserved for clergy—on a daily basis. Yet, these divine burdens always passed and one may say, she managed to function in the world in the most normal of ways, serving God's will of devotion and penance while working full-time in selfless service caring for the poor and sick in plague ravaged Genoa.

Catherine's published writings, compiled by her close friends and confessors, appeared some fifty years after her death. Her teachings and revelations were mostly dictated and written down by intimate others, primarily her confessor Father Marabotto, Battista Vernazza, and her close disciple, Ettore Vernazza. While there has been some discussion as to the origin of her writings, modern scholars are in agreement and attribute these works to her. Through the mystical grace, miracles, and ecstatic power of her divine voice, she has touched the heart of humanity. Catherine's selfless service and heroic virtue combined with the authenticity of miracles attributed to her, including receiving the stigmata and healing of a paralytic, led to her canonization by Pope Clement XII on April 30th, 1737. Her writings have been translated into over a dozen languages worldwide.

Saint Catherine of Genoa leaves behind two primary written works: *"The Spiritual Dialogues"* and *"The Treatise of Purgatory."* The latter, her most "famous" book, dictated to her confessor and spiritual director, Father Cattaneo Marabotto, describes her visions of the afterlife and the purification of souls. In addition, she shared her many spiritual insights and revelations with Battista Vernazza in letters, which were later compiled and published as *The Spiritual Dialogues*. *The Spiritual Dialogues* comprise an imagined, at times dramatic, profound, and meandering, conversation between the *Body, Soul, Self-Love, Humanity, and God,* revealing autobiographical elements of Catherine's struggle with reconciling earthly life and God's will.

I have chosen and edited several sections from *The Spiritual Dialogues* for reprint here, naming the book *Love's Guest,* as an invitation to focus on and share what feels to me like Saint Catherine of Genoa's Song of Divine

Love. When I first read these words, it felt like I was enveloped in a warm and comforting embrace, as if I was being held by a loving parent or close friend—carrying me to a place of deep mystery and surrender. I found this selection of her writings a beautiful symphony of Divine Love, with each word and phrase harmonizing to create a melody that inflames the heart and uplifts the soul.

I revised *Love's Guest* for the modern reader and tweaked some of the more archaic language and pronouns with the hope of offering a reading experience relevant to the diverse world of today. I changed words like "thou" to "you" and "man" to "humanity" to bestow a more gender-neutral feeling. I capitalized certain words sensing an emphasis on the divine quality of the word. Unequivocally, throughout the entire text, I strived to preserve the essence, passion, pathos and articulation of Saint Catherine's mystical experience. In addition, I offer a few annotated comments in key places of the text, marked by an endnote. At the end of the book you will find a workbook entitled, *Meditations for a New Understanding of Love,* comprised of quotations followed by questions for personal reflection and growth. I hope you will take your time moving through this section with pen and paper, allowing yourself a deeper experience of Saint Catherine's divine text.

When considering the inspiration and origin of Catherine's teachings it is important to note Catherine never formally studied any particular source. While the world she grew up in was rich in Catholic theology, all of her teachings and feelings for God appear to be her own spontaneous expressions of belief. These utterances came to her through devout meditations, prayer, and the Holy Spirit manifesting as an overwhelming ecstatic presence.

Saint Catherine's writings were completed long ago, and while you will find elsewhere the full volume of her works and detailed accounts of her life, you will note this is not a book about such details. This is a book offering a reflection on Divine Love inspired by a section from *The Spiritual Dialogues.* For anyone interested in a meticulous, complex study of Saint Catherine, her ideas, and her work, I recommend *The Mystical Element of Religion As Studied in Saints,* by Baron Friedrich Von Hugel.

In both of her seminal works, *The Treatise of Purgatory* and *The Spiritual Dialogues,* Catherine reveals a deep, resonant understanding, revelation, and philosophy of God in not only her life, but the spiritual life of humans. Her revelations express a connection between God's Love for humanity and our unique Spiritual Evolution. Ever present in her writings is an awareness of God's divine love drawing humans toward heaven, a quality she experienced as a constant truth, yet an unknowable element to the intellectual mind. Like all great Spiritual writing, Catherine revealed what her soul saw and heard, without the mind's filter.

Saint Catherine of Genoa inspires me to ask, what is the meaning of Divine Love in the world today?

There are many kinds of love: Love of family, partner, friend, culture, animals, travel, the arts, community, self-love—to name a few. There is also Love of God. For Catherine, Love is not only an expression of the divine, but also an elixir of life, ever present, ever "sweet," an elemental, untouchable knowledge that no human can contrive.

Catherine believed that love comes both to those willing to receive and to those who are not quite ready. This contrast encapsulates Saint Catherine's unique notion of "purgatory," which is also a metaphor for life. Life on earth, one may say, is a testing ground, day to day, to keep one's conscious faith and unconscious tendencies aligned with the will of God. As we do this, God is also drawing us forth, with boundless light, compassion, and acceptance—*whether we know it or not.* Saint Catherine's notion of purgatory, where human souls either suffer or complete their journey toward redemption and union with God, happens both on earth through the manner in which we live our life, and after death, with God's Divine Love always present. Thus, there is the potential for both suffering and joy on earth *and* after death, depending on our relationship with and awareness of God. I believe, as did Catherine, that the essence of our soul is ever aware. Divine Love is ever present in life and death.

In reading *Love's Guest,* you may discern Catherine's passion as a revelation of the Trinity. The Trinity is a classic Christian doctrine which claims we know the one God in three distinct ways as the Creator, Christ, and Holy Spirit. She appears to express Love as these three distinct voices of the Trinity throughout the text:

- Love as God, the Creator

God as the Creator is both our beginning and our end, which is expressed when Catherine explains, "Oh, Love, powerful and sweet, happy are those who are possessed by You, for You strengthen, defend, and preserve us from all ills of body and soul. You gently guide all things to their end and never abandon us. You are ever faithful. You give us light against the deceit of the devil, the malice of the world, and against ourselves, who are so full of self and so perverse."

- Love as Jesus, the human embodiment of God.

It is as if she is describing Jesus when she says, "Oh, Love, you accomplish the whole work of our salvation, which we neither know how to do nor are able to do without You."

- Love as the Holy Spirit, the presence of God within us.

Catherine captures the essence of the Holy Spirit when she writes, "Love is a Divine flame, and as material fire ever burns and consumes according to its nature; so, in humans the Love of God is, by its nature, ever working toward its end, and for its part never ceases to benefit and serve us whom it holds so dear."

Catherine moves between these three expressions of Love seamlessly, as her soul dictates. One may say, she is in the "flow" of revelation.

From birth through adulthood and old age, we trip through our errors and cultivate a relationship with Love through practice, devotion, and the inexplicable quality of "unknowing." As a wise man recently told me, "Love comes from above." Catherine saw that we have no control over love, except to get out of our own way—surrender and receive—and here is where we may find our hearts softening.

Catherine understood that we are always love's guest, should we be of open heart and accept love in our earthly home of Soul, Mind, and Body. In her divinely inspired writings you may find a certain magnitude of blessings—as if her words carry a certain charge of the blessed. Reading them for the first time, I experienced a kind of shower of Divine Love; something my intellectual mind could not understand—as if my heart understood something my mind could not.

*Love's Guest* is a manifesto for life on earth and for our relationship with the invisible. Herein, love is not merely a subject to be discussed; rather it's a profound feeling to be experienced—a dynamic force underpinning and holding together the nature of reality; a form within form—all of which "works in secret and subtlety, without show." Catherine notes, we often do not understand ourselves or our "condition," yet Love mysteriously remains. This Love is alive in the air we breathe and in the substance of our being, inescapable and essential to sustaining our life as individuals and as a community.

I present this small book as a token of my gratitude after stumbling across Catherine's words of divine inspiration. It seems nothing short of a miracle to receive these passages, written in the light and grace of Saint Catherine of Genoa's communion with God—and to feel them as they penetrate the marrow of our bones. This is the working of Grace: as we surrender, we receive. *Fiat voluntus tua.* Thy will be done.

Whether we comprehend Saint Catherine's words of Divine Love with our intellect or not—they offer a deep and transformative feeling of light and calm—a soul reflecting an immeasurable understanding, worthy of a Saint. It is my hope, as you read (and re-read) Catherine's words, you may also be inspired to inhale the blast of grace from which her words are born—and be healed, here and now.

May the blessings of these words change our common human threads toward the love Catherine knew so well. Whoever you are, wherever you find yourself in life, whatever you believe, may these words bring solace to your life and light to your heart. They flow from the deepest feelings of a human transformed and offer living proof that the waters of the divine may inspire our highest good.

It is my prayer that Catherine's voice awakens in you, however slight or imperceptible, the grace of God (Divinity, Source, Creator, Spirit) and that this grace moves you toward a renewed sense of personal meaning, with calm mind and body, inspiration and wonder.

Thank you, Saint Catherine of Genoa. Your blessings live on today.

MARC ARONOFF
March 3rd, 2023
Lenox, Massachusetts.

# LOVE'S GUEST

The Lord said, "Do you know who it is that employs my Love?"

You whose heart is pure and empty of every other love. When you find it, you remain content and satisfied, although you do not know my mode of operation nor your own condition because Love works in secret and subtly, without external show. Such a one is continually occupied, yet without occupation. We are bound, yet know not what holds us. We are in prison without an outlet.[2]

Oh Lord, what manner of Love is this?

What is this Love which is ever changing us from good to better, continually bringing us nearer to our end? And yet, as we approach, it more closely plunges us into an ever profounder ignorance of our situation. Humans in this state are kept alive by the rays of Love with which God pierces the heart and which return us to heaven in ardent sighs. If we did not find this relief, we would die through the vehemence of this fire.

Sometimes it so restrains us that we can neither speak nor sigh in order that its work may be more quickly done. But it does not hold us long in this condition because we cannot remain in it and live.

Oh, Love, the Soul that feels you begins even in this world to possess Eternal Life. But the Lord conceals this work even from its possessor, lest we should spoil it by making it our own.

Oh, Love, those who feel you, understand you not. Those who desire to comprehend you, cannot know you.[3]

Oh, Love, our life, our blessedness, our rest. Divine Love brings with it every good and banishes every evil. Oh, heart wounded with Divine Love, you are forever incurable and dying of this sweet wound. You enter upon never-ending life.

Oh, Fire of Love, what are you doing in humans?

You purify us as gold is purified by fire, and thus conduct us with you to that country and that end for which we are created. Love is a Divine flame, and as material fire ever burns and consumes according to its nature; so, in humans the Love of God is, by its nature, ever working toward its end, and for its part never ceases to benefit and serve us whom it holds so dear.

Those who do not know its power have but themselves to blame, since God never tires of doing good to us while He is in this life and has always the most tender Love for us.

Oh, Love, I can no longer be silent, and yet, I cannot speak as I desire of your sweet and gentle operation. For I am filled with Love, which inspires me with the wish to speak, but deprives me of the power to do so. Within myself, I speak with the heart and with the mind, but when I would pronounce the words, something checks me, and I find myself betrayed by this poor tongue.

I would be silent, but I cannot, for still, the instinct for speech urges me on.

If I could utter that Love of which my heart is full, I think that every other heart would be inflamed, however remote from Love it might be.

Before I leave this life, I long to speak once of this Love, to speak of it as I feel it within me—of its effects in me, and of what it requires of those into whom it is infused— and whom it fills to overflowing with a sweetness above all sweetness, and with an indescribable content so great that for it, one would willingly be burned alive. For God unites a certain zeal for this Love by the power of which we disregard all contradictions, however so great.

Oh, Love, powerful and sweet, happy are those who are possessed by You, for You strengthen, defend, and preserve us from all ills of body and soul. You gently guide all things to their end and never abandon us. You are ever faithful. You give us light against the deceit of the devil, the malice of the world, and against ourselves, who are so full of self and so perverse.

This Love is so illuminating and efficacious that it draws all imperfections from their secret caverns, that we may apply the remedy and purge ourselves from them.

This Love, which rules and governs our will in order
that it may grow strong and firm to resist temptation, so
occupies the affections and the intellect that they desire
nothing else. The memory is engrossed and the powers
of the Soul are satisfied so that Love remains her sole
possessor and inhabitant, and she allows nothing else to
enter there.

Love exhales a continual sweet perfume by which we suffer ourselves to be allured. And so powerful is this fragrance that, however great may be the torments through which we pass to salvation, there is no martyrdom we would not suffer gladly to attain it.

Oh, Love, no words of mine can express the sweetness and delight with which you fill the heart. It remains enclosed within, and by speaking, it is inflamed.

Whoever hears or reads these words without the sentiment of Love makes little account of them, and they pass by like the wind. But if I could express the joy, the pleasure, and the peace which it brings to the beloved heart, all people who hear or read these words would surrender without resistance. For it is so adapted to the human heart, that, at its first touch, it opens wide its door—although we can never receive this celestial gift until we are free from every other love.

If the heart receives but the smallest drop, it so earnestly desires to increase it that it rates as nothing all the goods of this world. With this Love, we conquer the evil habits which are a hindrance to us, and in its strength, we stand ever-ready to perform good deeds.

Oh, Love, with thy sweetness, you break the heart that is harder than adamant and melt it like wax in the fire.[4]

Oh, Love, you make great people esteem themselves as the least of the earth, and the richest, as the poorest.

Oh, Love, you cause wise men to appear as fools, and you take knowledge from the learned and give them an understanding surpassing all other understanding.

Oh, Love, you banish from the heart all melancholy, hardness, and natural inclinations, and all delight in worldly things.

Oh, Love, you make bad men good and artful men simple. You ingeniously deprive us of our free will so that we are content to be guided by you alone.

Oh, Love, your operations are alien to this earth, and therefore, you change us from earthly to celestial, depriving us of every human mode of operation, until we are unfit for earthly occupations.[5]

Oh, Love, you accomplish the whole work of our salvation, which we neither know how to do nor are able to do without You.

Oh, Love, your name is so sweet that it imparts sweetness to all things. Sweet is the mouth that names you, most of all when the words proceed from a heart full of your liquid sweetness, which makes us benign, meek, gracious, joyous, bountiful and ready, so far as may be to serve humanity.

Oh, Love, when by any way, you are able to penetrate the heart of humans with your gracious darts, however slight may be your flame, it is powerful enough to make us abandon all things else for you. This Love makes every affection and contradiction appear sweet.

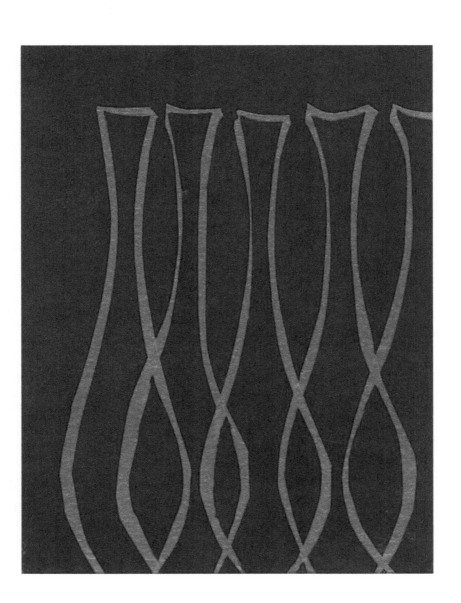

Oh, Love, what sweet quiet, and what quiet sweetness you bring forth. As you belong to all, the more you are diffused among creatures, so much the more fully is your will accomplished. The more we feel and comprehend your gentle warmth, the more we are inflamed with desire. We neither ask for any proof beyond this feeling, nor do we know how to give any other reason for it.

Love carries with it its own reason and will, and likewise, remains Lord of the whole human, subjecting us entirely to its will, according to its pleasure. And this work is wholly its own, for then its operations are affected through Love, in Love, and by Love.

By works done through Love, those works are understood which we perform through the love of God, when God gives us an instinctive desire to work for the benefit of ourselves or our neighbor. In this *first* state of love, God causes us to undertake many and various useful and necessary works which we perform with devout intention.

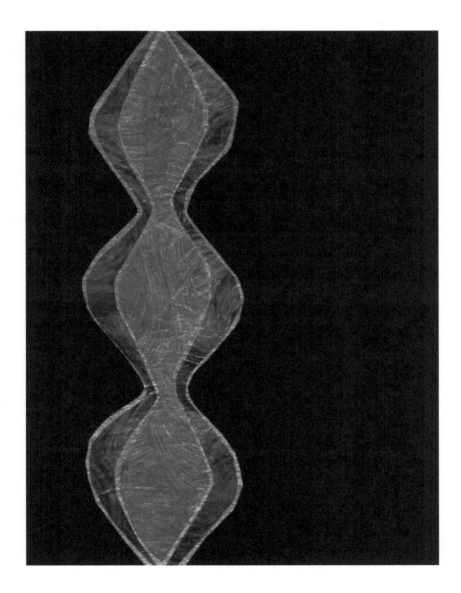

The works of the *second* state of Love are done in God. These are such as are done with no view either to the advantage to oneself or one's neighbor, but rest in God, with no motive in our actions. Here, we *persevere* in good works through the habit of virtues which we have formed, although God has deprived us of that share in them which give us aid and pleasure. This work is more perfect than the other, for in that, there are many motives which nourish both soul and body.

The works done by Love are more perfect than the other two because we have no part in them.

Love may so subdue and conquer us that we feel lost and left without the power to act. In this case, it is Love itself which works in us, and its works are works of Perfection, inasmuch as they are not wrought by human power and our works of sanctifying grace, and God accepts them all.

This sweet and pure Love takes possession of us, absorbs us, and deprives us of ourselves. It keeps possession of us and continually works within us solely for our benefit and advantage without any thought or care on our part.

Oh, Love, what a sweet companion and faithful guide
you are. Neither speech nor thoughts can do justice
to your excellence. Blessed is the heart possessed and
occupied by You.

Love makes us just, simple, pure, rich, wise, and
contented; and with its sweetness, it lessens every grief.

Oh, Love, all that is done through You is done with ease, with gladness and goodwill. And though the toil be difficult, Your sweetness tempers every trial.

Oh, the torment of working without Love; it is beyond belief. Love gives a sweet flavor to every food. If it is bad, Love makes it good. If good, Loves makes it better.

According to the grade and the capacity of the subject, God infuses love into the heart of humanity.[6]

Oh, how sweet a thing it would be to speak of this Love, if fitting words were found to express the delight with which it fills the heart. But because the Soul is immortal and capable of greater Love than it can feel in this life, on account of the weakness of the Body, which does not allow the Soul to support all that it desires, it remains ever craving, and in this life can never be fully satisfied.

Oh, Love, you fill the heart, but you are so great that it cannot contain you. It remains filled, but not satisfied. By the road of our heart, you take possession of us and permit none but yourself entrance. With a strong bond, you bind all the faculties of Soul and Body.

Oh, sweet servitude of Love which gives us freedom and contentment in this life and eternal blessedness in the other.

Oh, Love, your bonds are so sweet and so strong that they bind Angels and Saints together, and so firm and close that they are never broken.[7]

We who are bound by this chain are so united that we have but one Will and one aim, and all things are in common, both temporal and spiritual. In this Union, there is no difference between rich and poor, between nation and nation. All contradiction is excluded, for by this Love, crooked things are made straight and difficulties, reconciled.

All our words are heartfelt, glowing, and delightful—
so penetrating and in such subtle harmony with that
which inspires them—that they can be comprehended
only by those whose hearts are also united with God.
God alone comprehends them fully; the heart feels,
but understands not, and the work is that of God alone,
while the benefit belongs to humanity.[8]

This sweet love, so dear to me, which never leaves me to myself, is always speaking to me comforting me, inflaming me, and revealing to me some new and celestial beauty, so that my affection for it may become more and more ardent.

Love opens my heart and is ever making such gracious communications to it that it is wholly inflamed and dissolved in love; yet in particular can discern neither words, flames, nor love; the heart is seized, possessed, and held fast by a loving satisfaction.

O Love! the heart which You possess becomes peace of mind so great and so magnanimous, that it would rather suffer martyrdom to gain You than without You to be in possession of every other good in heaven or earth. Yet, this is beyond the comprehension of all who have not felt and tasted You.

O Love! you restore us to a true and perfect liberty, and make us masters of ourselves. We wish nothing but what God wishes and finds all things else a grave impediment.

O Love, I find no words to express Your joyous sway, Your strong and assured freedom, Your sweet and gentle goodness: but all that I could express would be unequal to what You would desire to say. I seek everywhere for loving words appropriate to that Love, and finds them nowhere; for Love and its effects are infinite, and my tongue is not only finite but very feeble, and is always dissatisfied and confused by its powerlessness to say what it desires.

All that can be said of love is nothing, for the further one advances, the less he knows; but the heart, filled and satisfied, seeks and desires nothing else but what it feels. All my words are heartfelt, glowing, and delightful, and so penetrating and in such subtle harmony with that which inspires them, that they can be comprehended only by those whose hearts are also united with God.

God only comprehends them fully; the heart feels but understands not, and the work is that of God alone, while the benefit belongs to humanity. But the intimate, amorous relation which God sustains in us is a secret between each of us and our heart.

A heart enamored of God is unconquerable, for God is its strength; hell does not frighten it nor heaven attract it, for it is so disposed that it receives all that happens as from the hand of God, remaining in immovable peace.

# R EFLECTION  G UIDE

## MEDITATIONS FOR A NEW
## UNDERSTANDING OF LOVE

While *Love's Guest* is meant to be read and re-read, taking your time to sense and feel any portion that resonates, allowing its fresh, warm wind to caress your face, here you are invited to take a few minutes to meditate, pray, and perhaps journal on a few selected passages with the questions that follow, offering a deeper opportunity for personal reflection.

As I am always interested in the meaning we make of words, I invite three brief definitions:

**MEDITATION**

Meditation is a non-denominational practice of cultivating stillness and awareness, moment-to-moment. Formally, this is accomplished by taking time to focus on an object of attention and to *return* to that focus (like the feeling of breathing), again and again, when distracted. This is a non-judgmental practice. When distracted with thoughts or sounds, the *returning* is an essential part of the meditation, leading eventually to a sustained presence of stillness and ease of wellbeing. Informally, meditation, or "mindful" awareness, is an opportunity to practice being in the world with an awake, non-judgmental presence, moment-to-moment. There are hundreds of formal meditations. The key is to find one that fits you and to try it out for a few months or years. Informally, your life is your practice.

**PRAYER**

Prayer is a tradition that invokes the Divine in our personal life through a sincere asking or being present; an opportunity to cultivate a personal relationship with God. Often seen as "petitionary," an asking for something, prayer is also a form of receiving God's blessing and being in God's presence, in deep surrender, devotion, and unknowing. There are many rituals and formal prayers, all of which are welcome here.

**CONTEMPLATIVE PRAYER**

Contemplative prayer combines mediation and prayer to deepen one's thoughts and questions around God, formally and informally.

*The Lord said, "Do you know who it is that employs my Love?" You whose heart is pure and empty of every other love.*

- What do you think Saint Catherine means by "empty of every other love"?
- What "other love" might you carry that may get in the way of "employing" the Lord's Love?

*Oh, Love, the Soul that feels you begins even in this world to possess eternal life. But the Lord conceals this work even from its possessor, lest we should spoil it by making it our own.*

In many mystical traditions, it is stated that God cannot be known by words or ideas. Like directions that point toward a destination, the directions are not the destination. Words are not the destination. Yet, we need the directions, to find the feeling for God. To feel Love is to begin to experience the eternal in life.

- How do you think we might "spoil it by making it our own?"
- Have you ever had the feeling you, (or your Soul), feels such Love as to possess eternal life? What is that like?

*Oh, Love, those who feel you, understand you not. Those who desire to comprehend you, cannot know you.*

- How might your mind or ego get in the way of knowing the Lord's Love?
- What are the different kinds of Love in your life today?

*Love is so illuminating and efficacious that it draws all imperfections from their secret caverns, that we may apply the remedy and purge ourselves from them.*

- What "imperfections" exist in you today that you might draw out from your "secret caverns" and remedy with Love?
- What are some of your secret caverns? What information do they have for you?
- Consider inviting in a certain Surrender and Gentleness as you explore this question.

*Oh, Love, you accomplish the whole work of our salvation, which we neither know how to do nor are able to do without You.*

Reflect or Pray on the following ideas and notice how this feels in the body:

- Love accomplishes the work of our Salvation.
- I surrender to God's Love.
- I do not need to know how to do the work of Salvation; I only need to surrender and allow Love to do its work.
- I am willing to enter into and accept a certain trust and surrender, allowing Love to heal me without human logic or control.

*This Love, which rules and governs our will in order that it may grow strong and firm to resist temptation, so occupies the affections and the intellect that they desire nothing else.*

Reflect or Pray on the experience:
- Love occupies my intellect completely, and I desire nothing else.
- Imagine and allow the feeling of God's Love to occupy every cell in your body. Notice how that feels.

*Oh, Love, you make bad men good and artful men simple. You ingeniously deprive us of our free will so that we are content to be guided by you alone.*

Reflect or Pray on the questions:
- What would life be like if I allowed myself to be guided by God alone?
- How does this affect my free will?

*Imagine your "God Chord," ever-wise, ever-true, running through your spine, and imagine yourself always connected to God.*[9]

- Imagine a particular problem in your life.
- Imagine experiencing your God Chord and *No Separation* from God.
- How does that problem feel now, in the Light of God?

Surrender sometimes clarifies what action is needed.

*Love may so subdue and conquer us that we feel lost and left without the power to act . . .*

*This sweet and pure Love takes possession of us, absorbs us, and deprives us of ourselves. It keeps possession of us and continually works within us solely for our benefit and advantage, without any thought or care on our part.*

Reflect or Pray on the following ideas:
- Love continually works within me solely for my "benefit and advantage."
- There is no separation between myself and God: We are One Creative Divine Expression.

## THE LOVE MEDITATION

1. Sitting upright or lying down, close your eyes or relax them half-closed, and breathe with your belly, noticing it rising and falling. Allow your hands to relax how they want, palms up or down, or resting gently on your tummy, legs, or by your side. Take a few minutes to breathe with awareness, allowing the belly to rise and fall. Pay attention to the feeling of your belly rising and falling.

2. Visualize the numbers 10-0 in your imagination, moving backwards. See each number appear and disappear, from 10-0. Let that go. Notice how you feel. Breathe for a few seconds.

3. Now, take your time and notice your right hand—in particular, the weight of your hand, curl of the fingers, temperature, texture of the material the hand is touching. Take a moment to notice your right hand. Now, notice your left hand in the same manner. Now, notice both hands simultaneously. Notice your body as a whole, breathing, as if you are a witness. Observe yourself breathing for a few a moments.

4. Now, let your body breathe how it wants and notice the feeling of doing **nothing.** Allow yourself to do **nothing. Nothing** to get. Nowhere to go. Notice how **nothing** feels. Hold onto no particular thought. Do **nothing.** Notice how **nothing** feels.

5. After a few minutes of breathing and doing **nothing,** you will notice that a "good feeling" arises or bubbles up in your awareness. This good feeling may be slight. Perhaps you may experience a sense of light or joy, bliss or love, ease of well-being, or gratitude. However slight, stay with the good feeling.

6. Let the good feeling in you bubble up and occupy your awareness. Rest in the good feeling. If you are distracted with thought, come back to noticing your right hand, left hand, both hands, body breathing as a whole, then the feeling of doing **nothing.**

7. Bathe in the good feeling; stay with the good feeling as long as you would like.

8. Now, imagine and feel a time when you were loved. Allow that image and feeling to occupy your whole body. Imagine and experience the feeling of being loved. If nothing comes to you, be creative—perhaps

surround yourself with white Light or imagine an Angel holding you. Perhaps imagine you are with a pet that loves you. Remember or imagine a time of love. Allow that memory to permeate your being.

9. Shift your focus now and notice your body as a whole, breathing effortlessly. Simply abide in quiet awareness, moment-to-moment. If the feeling of love is present, stay with it.

10. If it feels right, you may invite a prayer at this time. Anything you want. Perhaps ask a question for guidance. Listening to this quiet, I sometimes ask, "What is the one thing I need to know or do now?" Do not think about any right answers. Sit quietly with any feelings or information you receive. Take a few moments to feel your body as a whole, breathing effortlessly. When you are ready, slowly open your eyes and look around the room. How do you feel?

11. Feel free to adapt this meditation in part or whole, as you would like. Make it you own.

*Oh, Love, all that is done through You is done with ease, with gladness and goodwill. And though the toil be great, Your sweetness tempers every trial.*

- Life is full of great toil, trial and error; yet Catherine invites us to see that all that is done through Love is done with ease, gladness, surrender, and goodwill. Yes, it is possible to feel with the heart of Saint Catherine of Genoa.
- May this be our practice—Our meditation. Our choice. Our prayer.

# AFTERWORD

## BROTHER PAUL QUENON

Love. What is there to say about it? Everything. Nothing. To open your mouth is futility; it is rapture. Every word is truth, every word false. It takes a saint bold enough to risk both. At best, we can stand at a distance and listen to Saint Catherine. The empty space on these pages shows this kind of discretion. Likewise, Jan Richardson's bold images of simple design alone are appropriate here; primal colors without pretense, forms that speak themselves with no attempt at being other.

Love deserves words, if any, that compel by intimating what one knows within oneself already: Words which expand one beyond a capacity you might recognize as your own; words that succeed by recognizing their own inadequacy. Love expands your words, exaggerates your words—it dazzles and enchants; reduces words down to a minimum—it humbles and simplifies. Every tactic is fair game; no tactic is respectful, that is nothing other than authenticity and renunciation of tactic. It takes a saint to do this.

Love diffuses itself. It wants to find itself everywhere, in every heart, tameless, contagious. Love is subtle, traceless, arrives uninvited, enters by innuendos and implications, takes residence where it always belonged. A heart is not home until occupied by love. All it takes is a spark, all it ignites is an inflammation unto wholeness. Holiness is wholeness; holiness is poverty dispossessed of everything but love.

Love is bewilderment. Who is the one loving? Is it me or is it love loving in me? Bliss means to be possessed by love greater than myself, myself made more than what I ever was; possessed by sublime bewilderment where I finally recognize myself, myself for what I always was but never recognized. Such intimacy is nameless, yet nothing has ever been closer to me than this, so close as to be unreachable—a fragrance elusive and inescapable, detected then faded, filling the senses then fully absorbed as one's own.

A saint is one who has become love—a love that has forgotten about being a saint and can only be love. A saint surrenders to being nothing but love in whatever circumstances, trivial or great, obscure, and unremarkable, or public and unmistakable. The less evident a circumstance might be, the better; for their it becomes obvious that love is something beyond the saint—obvious especially to the saint.

A monk or a hermit abides in the inexpressible. That is one way of being true to love. St. Catherine, of Genoa, on the other hand, was uniquely possessed by love. At times, we know this apostle of love was unable not to speak of love. It burned her painfully and at the same time, she confessed it a supreme bliss unlike anything she ever knew. And all this she lived through while collaborating in remarkable works of charity.

One must first hear and listen to the inner stirrings of love, and then find ones true direction in life. These pages contain the quintessence of such stirrings.

**BROTHER PAUL QUENON** O.C.S.O. has been a monk of the Abbey of Gethsemani for 64 years. His novitiate formation was under Thomas Merton. His latest book, *How to Be,* is a collection of letters with national journalist Judith Valente on matters of mutual interest. His memoir *In Praise of the Useless Life* received the Catholic Press award for memoirs. His latest book of poetry is *Amounting to Nothing,* and a selected volume of poetry is found in *Unquiet Vigil.*

# ANNOTATED ENDNOTES

[1] *Thomas Merton describes these saints as "complete and simple signs of contradictions to worldliness and system, and convention, and prejudiced interest . . . In them you see clearly and movingly revealed what is not to be a mere rebel, but what is to be obedient to God as a sign of mercy, a revelation of truth and of power . . . meek and submissive instruments of God." (p. xv)*

Merton, Thomas. *Journals of Thomas Merton: Turning Toward the World* Volume 4. Ed. by Victor A Kramer, San Francisco: Harper Collins, 1996, p. 100.

[2] *The Lord said, "Do you know who it is that employs my Love?" You whose heart is pure and empty of every other love. When you find it, you remain content and satisfied, although you do not know my mode of operation nor your own condition, because Love works in secret and subtlety, without external show. Such a one is continually occupied, yet without occupation. We are bound, yet know not what holds us. We are in prison without an outlet. (p. 3)*

Here, as in several other moments, Saint Catherine reveals an autobiographical window into the depth of her struggles. It is possible at certain times the revelation of God in her life was so overwhelming, it felt like a prison.

[3] *Oh, Love, those who feel you, understand you not. Those who desire to comprehend you, cannot know you. (p. 5)*

As in many religious traditions, it is believed, as Saint Catherine knows, the expression of God cannot be revealed in words. The concept is simply too big for the human intellect. One may say, the most we can hope for are glimpses—the experience of God revealed through feeling, vision, and mystery—and still, no words can touch this revelation. Yet, one must also acknowledge, Saint Catherine comes as close as any human in expressing God in words.

[4] *Oh, Love, with thy sweetness, you break the heart that is harder than adamant and melt it like wax in the fire. (p. 20)*

This reminds me of a lecture I attended led by a Trappist monk. He expressed that there are two ways to grow old: We will either grow hard, brittle, and malcontent in mind, body, and heart, or we will soften in faith and love. I am aware this is easier said than done, as old age and illness may bring remorse and bitterness. Yet, even here, Love may find its way. And, it is often said, how we live our life will be how we age and die.

[5] *Oh, Love, your operations are alien to this earth, and therefore, you change us from earthly to celestial, depriving us of every human mode of operation, until we are unfit for earthly occupations. (p. 23)*

I imagine, this capacity for Love to change humans from "earthly to celestial" would be something Saint Catherine experienced personally during her struggles to translate her revelations into day-to-day accomplishments, sometimes feeling "unfit for earthly occupations." There is a sense of the supernatural here, an essential ingredient to experiencing God, unfiltered, without doubt or resistance. Yet, Saint Catherine appears to have remained grounded in her earthly life, consistently showing up for work at the Genoa Hospital attending with deep respect to the poor and infirm. This speaks to the human dance of accomplishing daily tasks while steeped in an awareness of the Holy Spirit.

[6] *According to the grade and the capacity of the subject, God infuses love into the heart of humanity. (p. 36)*

We each walk this earth according to our "capacity" to understand and dispel "ignorance" in relation to life, love, and God. Ignorance, in this sense, is not a lack of knowledge or smarts, but a misperception we are separate from God and thus speaking, acting, and doing from an "egoic" identity. The question is, how willing are we to cultivate a personal relationship with God, through trial and error and, according to our capacity, receive that essential Divine water that nourishes the seeds of awakening? This is an intention as much as an active purpose.

*7 Oh, Love, your bonds are so sweet and so strong that they bind Angels and Saints together, and so firm and close that they are never broken. (p. 40)*

With this passage, I sense Saint Catherine is experiencing the spiritual nature of life, where Angels and Saints bind together for Love and human evolution. This is where humanity has one aim—the realization of God on earth: *As above, So below.* This aspect of our spiritual life is a distinction where ego falls away and "all contradiction is excluded." Here, at work and at play, we may experience the sweet nature of Union with God's purpose on earth. Here, there is *No Separation* from God. In this state we may approach the sometimes dark side of life with forgiveness, faith, and prayer, revealing Light and Grace in every corner of darkness. And if we cannot get it quite right, that is also part of the divine plan and prayer for humans. Like a meditation practice, this prayer will come in and out of our awareness. When we lose focus, we are invited to start over without judgement, vowing to do our best, moment-to-moment.

*8 All our words are heartfelt, glowing, and delightful, so penetrating and in such subtle harmony with that which inspires them, that they can be comprehended only by those whose hearts are also united with God. God alone comprehends them fully; the heart feels, but understands not, and the work is that of God alone, while the benefit belongs to humanity. (p. 41)*

Saint Catherine speaks of God within us. Only those whose hearts are united with God understands them. This is God's actualization through Humankind,

The *Imago Dei*—the image of God in humans. As humans are made in the Likeness of God (Genesis 1:26), it is our God-nature, ever present and ever wise, that understands Saint Catherine's words, as if the ego steps out the way and lets the Soul comprehend. It is inevitable that God cares for Humankind. If we could only get out of our own harmful ways of being and thinking, and listen with our hearts to our God-nature more often, what might the world look like?

[9] *Imagine your God Chord, ever-wise, ever-true, running through your spine, and imagine yourself always connected to God. (p. 58)*

Our "God Chord," is an idea that I use while working with clients and leading retreats that connects us at all times to our higher wisdom and a feeling of God in the mind/body.

# THE GLOW

Everyone who delights in some act
of devotion
can't bear to miss it,
even for a short while.
That disappointment and grief
are worth a hundred prayers.

What is a formal prayer compared
to the glow of humble longing?

RUMI
MATHNAWI II